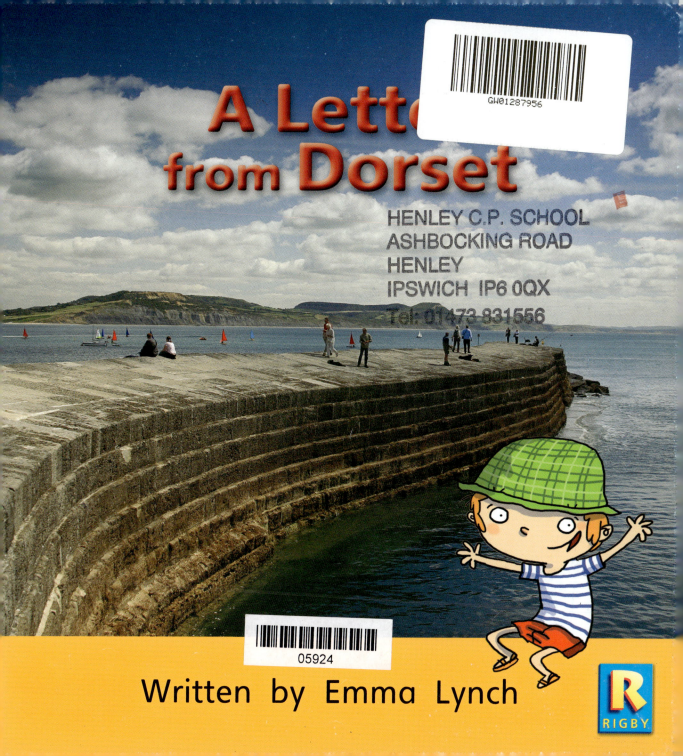

A Letter from Dorset

Written by Emma Lynch

Dear Gran!
How are you? We are all well.

Gran
2 Hill Top Road
Blackpool

This summer we are visiting Dorset.

The caravan park is near the coast.

We can hear the gulls at night.

A funfair was on in the town.

I went on the bumper cars. Bert was afraid to go near them.

We went to a farm for kids.
The farmer let us feed the goats.

Bert was afraid to go near them!

We got fish and chips for dinner.

It was the best! We sat on the sand until the sun set.

We went on a fossil hunt.
I got a fossil fish.

The fossil was in a rock.
I am sure that Bert was afraid of it.

We went crabbing, too.
It was the best!
I got a crab in my bucket.

We had a look at the crab,
then we let it go.
Yes, Bert was afraid of it!

Hugs and kisses from all of us.
Lara, Bert, Mum and Dad.